You must come away
to some lonely place
and rest for a while.

– Mark 6:31

COME AND SEE

A Pilgrim's Picture Book

Shrine Of The
Most Blessed
Sacrament

Dear  Pilgrim,

Welcome to the Shrine of the Most Blessed Sacrament. The prayers and photographs in this book will re-create for you the experience of a pilgrimage to this Temple of the Divine Child Jesus. It is my prayer that you will receive much light and many graces from this pilgrimage.

Perhaps the question pilgrims most frequently ask is, "How did it all begin?" As unlikely as it may seem, the Lord used an ordinary business trip to manifest His Will. In 1995, EWTN (Eternal Word Television Network) planned to start a Spanish television network for Latin America where growing numbers of Catholics were losing their faith. So I traveled to South America with two of my Sisters to ask Bishops and Nuncios to help EWTN make programs in the different Spanish dialects.

One of the countries we visited was Colombia. Whenever I travel, I always try to attend Holy Mass each day at a Shrine or other holy place, so that even a business trip can become at least partially a pilgrimage. In Bogotá, a wonderful Salesian Priest, Father Juan Pablo Rodriguez, brought us to see the Sanctuary of the Divine Infant Jesus. I was very surprised by the contrast between the poverty of the people and the beauty of their Basilica. The Church was so packed that we had to attend Mass outside in a large courtyard with thousands of other people. After Mass, Father showed us a medallion of the Priest who had founded the original Church, Father John Rizzo — the same name as my own father!

Father Rizzo was an Italian Salesian Priest who came to Bogotá in the early 1900's just to take care of these very poor people. Father Rizzo had great devotion to the Sacred Childhood of Jesus and bought a statue to encourage the people to pray to the Divine Child. As time went on, this statue proved to be miraculous. Whenever the people were in great need, Father Rizzo would pray to the Child Jesus, Who performed many miracles from feeding the hungry to healing the sick.

Then Father Juan Pablo brought us to see the miraculous statue of the Child Jesus. We went into a small Shrine that was full of people. There was no room for us in front of the statue, so I stood at the side. I was looking up at His profile and praying, when suddenly the miraculous statue became alive and turned around towards me. He had the most beautiful eyes I had ever seen! Then the Child Jesus said to me with the voice of a young boy, ***"Build Me a Temple and I will help those who help you."*** I was awestruck! I began to cry at His beauty and simplicity.

When we arrived back home from South America, I told the Sisters what happened in Bogotá. Where would we start? What would we do? I didn't know, but I supposed that the first step was to look for land. We searched everywhere for several months. Finally the real estate agent said there was one last place to look.

The moment we stepped on this property, I felt the Presence of God very strongly. Later we discovered that the original deed had been signed on August 2, the Solemnity of Our Lady of the Angels, which is the Patronal Feast Day of our Monastery.

> *"He designed it, He built it, and He paid for it."*
> — Mother M. Angelica

Once we had the land, the "Temple" had to be designed. I didn't understand what the word "Temple" meant. I knew there were Jewish Temples, but I'd never heard of a *Catholic* Temple. It wasn't until we went to Rome, sometime after the South American trip, that the Lord showed me what He meant by a "Temple". As we were leaving Saint Peter's Basilica, I turned around and saw these words: *"This Temple was consecrated . . . ."* Now I knew there was such a thing as a Catholic Temple. I was overjoyed.

To me, this Temple is a miracle. The miracle is not so much that the Temple was built, but *how* it was built. From the very start, it was the Lord's own doing — He designed it, He built it, and He paid for it. God's Providence is so awesome. We had no money to build, but we never tried to raise funds, and EWTN had no participation in paying for any part of the Temple. This was totally a project of Our Lady of the Angels Monastery.

The Child Jesus kept His promise: *". . . and I will help those who help you."* He inspired people we didn't know and who didn't know each other. The entire edifice — Church, Piazza, Monastery, Enclosure Wall, roads — everything was paid for by five families who wanted their donations to remain anonymous. The bills would come in, and these five families would pay them. To me, that's a great miracle of God's Providence. Never in my wildest dreams did I think the Temple would be so beautiful. My Sisters and I thought it should be very simple, but God had other plans. As I would give reports to the families, things would evolve far differently from the architect's original design. For example, I told one benefactor that we were going to use tile for the Church floor, and she replied, "Oh no, you must have marble." I said, "It's very expensive." She answered, "I know. I'll pay for it." It was the same with every other detail of the Shrine. I took all of this as God's Will. These five families were so generous, and wanted to build something beautiful for the Lord.

And so this is truly a Church that God has built — a real Temple, a place where people can come and rest their souls, renew their faith, and give themselves an opportunity to receive the graces and the peace, the forgiveness and the Mercy that only God can give.

It is my hope and the hope of all my Sisters that you will be blessed by this pilgrimage. We pray that you will be led to a deeper love for the Child Jesus and the Holy Eucharist, that your soul will be refreshed, and that your spiritual life will be renewed. As you journey back into the world, may the memory of this holy place bring you peace.

Prayerfully,

Mother M. Angelica

Mother M. Angelica

Pilgrimage Song

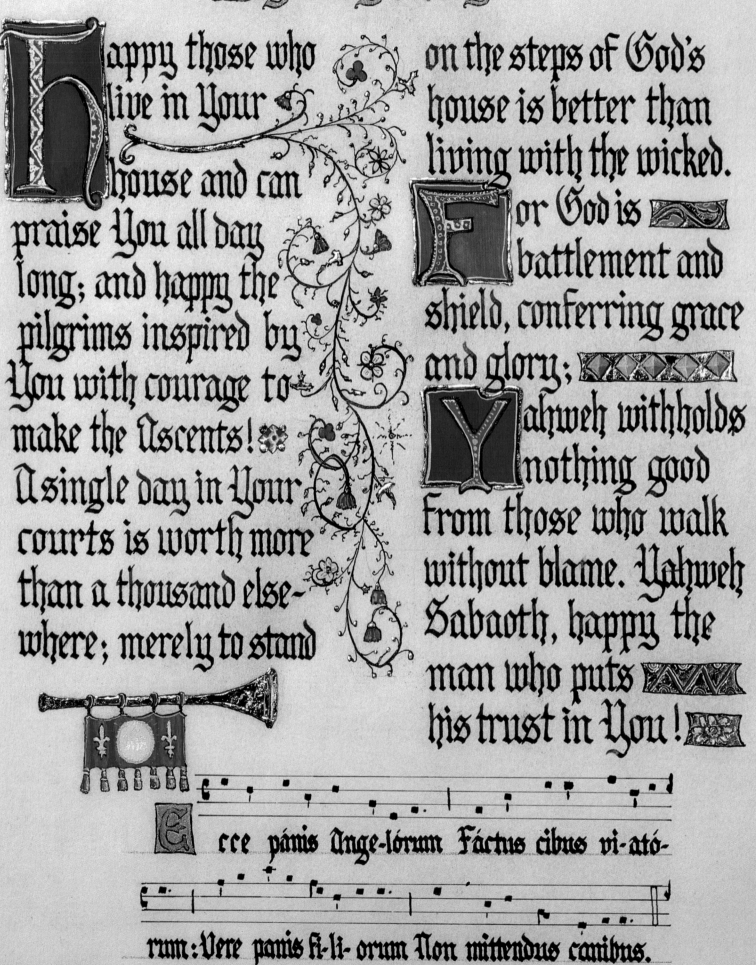

Happy those who live in Your house and can praise You all day long; and happy the pilgrims inspired by You with courage to make the Ascents! A single day in Your courts is worth more than a thousand else-where; merely to stand on the steps of God's house is better than living with the wicked. **F**or God is battlement and shield, conferring grace and glory; **Y**ahweh withholds nothing good from those who walk without blame. Yahweh Sabaoth, happy the man who puts his trust in You!

Ecce panis Ange-lorum Factus cibus vi-ato-rum: Vere panis fi-li- orum Non mittendus canibus.

Come and See . . .

From the very day of Consecration on December 19, 1999 until the present, constant streams of people have come to visit the Shrine of the Most Blessed Sacrament. Some visitors come out of mere curiosity, while others come with heartfelt devotion. Some come to see the architecture, while others come to adore the Lord. Regardless of the reason for their visit, after passing through the bronze Great Doors into Jesus' Eucharistic Presence, something happens. No one is left unmoved.

Every pilgrim, coming with a sincere intention, has been touched in a profound way. Many fall to their knees before the awesome majesty of Our Lord's Real Presence — Body, Blood, Soul, and Divinity — in the Most Blessed Sacrament. Others, visibly moved by the beauty of His Temple, are overcome by an intense awareness of His Presence.

The magnificent Monstrance, the pure white marble in the Sanctuary, the inlaid gold "Sanctus, Sanctus, Sanctus" on the steps leading up to the Altar, the devotional Stained-glass Windows, and the many other beautiful features of the Shrine, all evoke a response within the soul . . . to give love in return for Love.

More than a mere emotional experience, a pilgrimage to the Shrine of the Most Blessed Sacrament is an encounter with the Living God — it is a meeting between the soul and Jesus. This "meeting" inflames the soul with a desire to follow Him, for He is "the Way, the Truth, and the Life."

"They said to Him, 'Rabbi, where dwellest Thou?' He said to them, 'Come and see.' They came and saw where He was staying; and they stayed with Him that day . . ." (John 1:38-39).

"You must come away to some lonely place and rest for a while" (Mark 6:31). Why come to a "lonely" place? The goal of a pilgrimage is a personal meeting between God and the soul. At this intimate meeting, nothing else may be permitted to intrude — not the cares of this world, nor our disordered desires, not even our daydreams and distractions. The soul must spend this time truly alone with God.

To help the pilgrim set aside the cares and concerns of everyday life, the spacious Piazza provides a setting for recollection and preparation before entering into the Eucharistic Presence of the Lord. The Piazza changes one's focus from what was left behind, to what the Lord wants to give: Himself and His Love.

O Lord Jesus, I have come to this holy place as a pilgrim.
Help me to ponder what it is that must be cast away from my heart and soul
before I enter into Your Presence. Lead me to begin a new life, one that is
truly spiritual. Prepare me for the transformation that
You want to effect within my soul. Amen

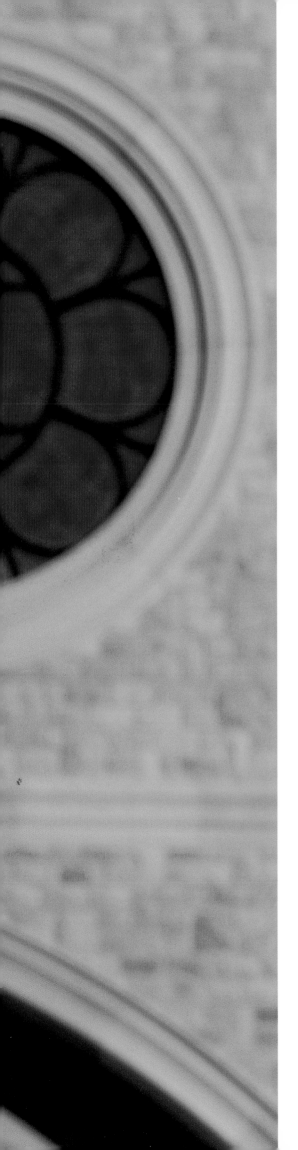

The Monument of El Divino Niño Jesús is the centerpiece of the Piazza. In utter simplicity, the Child Jesus holds His Heart in His hand, inviting us to accept His Love and imitate His Childlikeness.

Engraved in four languages on the steps leading up to the Monument is a message of hope for everyone:

". . . And a little Child shall lead them"
(Isaiah 11:6).

May this statue of the Child Jesus inflame the hearts of parents with love for their children and be a deterrent to women who are considering an abortion, to change their minds and hearts to choose life.

"And He took a child, and put him in the midst of them; and taking him in His arms, He said to them, 'Whoever receives one such child in My name receives Me; and whoever receives Me, receives not Me but Him Who sent Me.'"
— Mark 9:36-37

Ever since the Middle Ages, bells have been considered an essential part of every Church. Their purpose is to call the Faithful to the Holy Sacrifice of the Mass and to sound the funeral toll. They also ring three times a day for the Angelus, a traditional prayer in honor of the Incarnation of Our Lord. In Monasteries, bells are also used to summon the Monks or Nuns to their Chapel for the recitation of the Divine Office (the

Liturgy of the Hours).

Because of their role of calling the Faithful to prayer, it became customary to bless Church bells in a special ceremony resembling Baptism. In this ceremony, each bell, adorned with a crown of flowers and vested with a custom-made "stole", is blessed with Holy Water, anointed with Holy Chrism Oil, and given a name.

The Shrine's 110-foot bell tower houses a carillon of fourteen cast-bronze bells, eleven of which are over a hundred years old. The largest bell, Divino Niño Jesús, tolls the hours of the day and the Angelus. Names of the other bells include Most Sacred Heart of Jesus, Our Lady of the Most Holy Rosary, and Saint Michael the Archangel.

*"A single day in Your courts is worth more
than a thousand elsewhere; merely to stand on the steps
of God's House is better than living with the wicked."*
— Psalm 84:10

There are seven steps leading up to the Portico of the Temple. The number seven is symbolic in Sacred Scripture — most notably the seven days of creation in Genesis and the Seven Gifts of the Holy Spirit in Isaiah.

As a pilgrim reaches the threshold he instinctively looks up, as all the elements of the facade draw the eyes

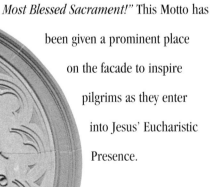

Heavenward. Above the bronze Great Doors appears the Motto of the Poor Clare Nuns of Perpetual Adoration: *"Adoremus in Aeternum Sanctissimum Sacramentum"* — *"Let us adore for all Eternity the Most Blessed Sacrament!"* This Motto has been given a prominent place on the facade to inspire pilgrims as they enter into Jesus' Eucharistic Presence.

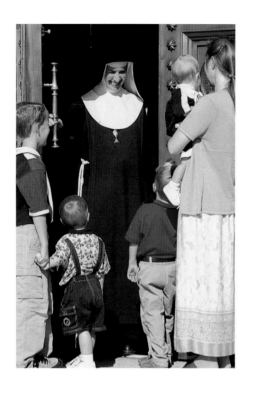

"Ask and it will be given to you; search, and you will find; knock, and the door will be opened to you."

— Matthew 7:7

The bronze Great Doors of the Shrine provide the pilgrim with fourteen meditations on the life of the Blessed Virgin Mary. Each panel invites the pilgrim to unite his joys and sorrows to the Joys and Sorrows of Mary, the Mother of Our Saviour. By meditating on these images, the pilgrim is encouraged to repeat Our Lady's unwavering *"Yes"* to the Will of God in the present moment. The intricate beauty of the Great Doors also offers a glimpse of the "Glory of the Lord" which shines with splendor inside the magnificent Temple.

The very act of opening the door symbolizes the pilgrim's willingness to open his heart to all the graces the Lord desires to give, especially the grace of conversion. How generously the Lord will bestow His graces upon those who open these Doors while pondering with love and confidence Our Lady's words: *"Behold the handmaid of the Lord; be it done to me according to thy word"* (Luke 1:38).

The prayerful meditations on the next four pages will help prepare for the pilgrim's entrance into the Temple.

The Seven Joys of Mary

1. THE ANNUNCIATION

O Mary, grant me

a share in your Faith

and Hope, that I may

accept the treasures

that the Father desires

to bestow upon me.

3. THE NATIVITY

Sweet Mother, give me the

grace to take my place

with the Shepherds, that I

may tell Jesus of my love

and gratitude.

2. THE VISITATION

Holy Mary, obtain for me

the graces I need

to magnify the Lord

through humility

in dealing with

my neighbour.

5. THE FINDING OF JESUS IN THE TEMPLE

*Dear Mother, with you I
rejoice in the finding of
Jesus in the Temple.
Grant that I may never
lose Him through sin.*

7. THE ASSUMPTION AND CORONATION

*My Queen and my Mother!
Obtain for me all the
graces I need to enter His
Kingdom and be crowned
with the unfading
crown of holiness.*

4. THE ADORATION OF THE MAGI

*Kind Mother, place
within my heart the
reverence of the Magi
as they prostrated
themselves in Adoration
before your Son.*

6. MARY REJOICES AT JESUS' RESURRECTION

*O Blessed Mother,
you rejoiced to see Jesus
after His Resurrection.
Help me to grow in the
virtue of Hope.*

The Seven Sorrows of Mary

1. The Prophecy of Simeon

Most Sorrowful Mother,

share with me

that courage which

enabled you to accept

the prophecies of Simeon

with trust and

abandonment.

2. The Flight into Egypt

Sweet Mary, help me

to surrender to

the Will of God,

even in the midst of

darkness and fear.

3. The Loss of Jesus in the Temple

Kind Mother, help me to

understand the agony of

your Pure Heart as you

searched for your Son

Jesus for three days.

5. JESUS DIES ON THE CROSS

Dear Mother, grant that I may always be united to you, as you stood beneath the Cross of Jesus.

7. JESUS IS LAID IN THE TOMB

Our Lady of Sorrows, I desire to comfort you as they roll the stone in front of the Tomb.

Help me to imitate your Faith, your Hope, and your Love for Jesus.

4. MARY MEETS JESUS ON THE WAY TO CALVARY

O Blessed Mother, help me to think of that glance between you and Jesus — the glance that said, "Let Us offer this to the Father for the salvation of souls."

6. JESUS IS TAKEN DOWN FROM THE CROSS

O Mary, you held the lifeless Body of your Son and beheld the Wounds that my sins inflicted.

Help me to live so as never to wound Him again.

We adore Thee,
O Lord Jesus Christ,
here and in all the Churches
of the whole world,
and we bless Thee,
because by Thy Holy Cross
Thou hast redeemed
the world,
and because
Thou givest Thyself
to us in the
Most Blessed Sacrament.

Above the bronze Minor Doors are Lunettes picturing the two great Saints of Assisi, Francis and Clare. They are the Founders of the Franciscan Religious Orders. The Nuns who dwell within Our Lady of the Angels Monastery, which adjoins the Shrine, belong to one branch of the Franciscan family — the Poor Clares of Perpetual Adoration. It is their constant, hidden presence in the Temple which enables the Most Blessed Sacrament to remain in the Monstrance day and night, all through the year. The Nuns totally consecrate their lives to the Adoration and Worship of Jesus.

The Poor Clares of Perpetual Adoration are a Contemplative Religious Order that is unique in the Church. The Order was founded in Paris, France in 1854 by Mother Marie de Ste. Claire Bouillevaux. She united the Franciscan form of Gospel living with Perpetual Adoration of the Most Blessed Sacrament in the spirit of thanksgiving. Mother Bouillevaux was inspired by the Gospel account of Jesus healing the ten lepers, of whom only one returned to give Him thanks (Luke 17:12-19). There are more than twenty Monasteries of this Pontifical Order in seven countries, including Europe, India, and the United States.

Upon entering the Temple, pilgrims
are awestruck by the radiant beauty of the
Monstrance and the awesome Majesty of
His Eucharistic Presence. The Sacred
Host which we adore is the Body, Blood,
Soul and Divinity of Jesus, consecrated
during the Holy Sacrifice of the Mass.
It is this Real Presence of Jesus that
inspires the soul to a reverent
genuflection as an outward act
of Worship. The heart of the
pilgrim is enkindled with the
desire to remain with Jesus for
a time of silent Adoration
and prayer.

A special candle, called
a "Sanctuary Lamp", constantly
burns within the Sanctuary, indicating
the reservation of the Consecrated Hosts
within the closed Tabernacle. This flickering
candle evokes in the depths of the soul the
awareness that Jesus is truly there awaiting us. Like
the Sanctuary Lamp, the pilgrim's heart yearns to remain
continually in the Presence of Our Lord.

And the glory of the Lord fills the Temple!

"...day and night they never cease to
sing, 'Holy, holy, holy is the Lord
God Almighty, Who was
and is and is to come!'"
— Revelation 4:8

The time of pilgrimage is a special opportunity to refocus our spiritual vision on "the one thing necessary". The Holy Angels are always ready to remind and encourage us to "love the Lord your God with all your heart, with all your soul, and with all your mind" (Matthew 22:37).

The Angel Windows in the Temple give an example of how to do this. Each window is oriented with the Angel's gaze focused on the Most Blessed Sacrament. Like the Angels we must turn our gaze to the Lord, so that we may accomplish God's Holy Will.

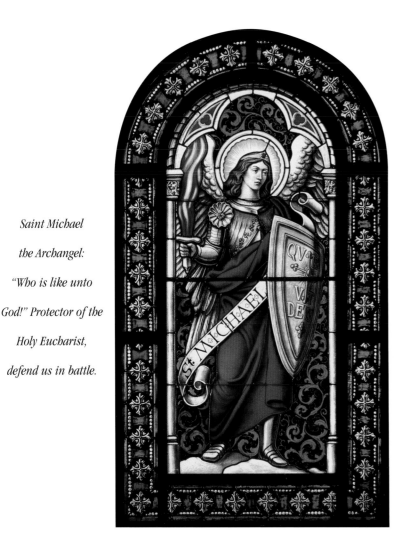

Saint Michael the Archangel: "Who is like unto God!" Protector of the Holy Eucharist, defend us in battle.

Saint Gabriel the Archangel: "Strength of God". Protector of the Sacrament of Baptism, intercede for us at the Throne of Divine Mercy.

"See that you despise not one of these little ones:
for I say to you, that their Angels in Heaven always see
the Face of My Father Who is in Heaven."
— Matthew 18:10

*Saint Raphael
the Archangel:
"Medicine of God".
Protector of the
Sacrament of
Penance, heal our
spiritual and bodily
infirmities.*

*First Choir:
O Ardent Seraphim,
inflame me
and all men
with your purest
angelic love,
that with you we may
love God here on earth
and one day for all
Eternity in Heaven*

*Second Choir:
O Bright Cherubim,
defend us from
the enemy, that our
hearts may always
be pure and
undefiled Temples of
the Most Holy Trinity.*

*Third Choir:
O Sublime Thrones,
inspire and direct
the hearts of men
so that many
Saints may arise
in every nation
and every
Religious Community.*

Fourth Choir:
O Supreme Dominations,
illuminate the minds
of men and inflame
their hearts, that soon
there may be
but one fold
and one Shepherd.

Fifth Choir:
O Heavenly Virtues,
assist us in the
most important task
of our purification,
that we may
never fear the sacrifices
necessary to grow in
holiness and virtue.

Eighth Choir:
O Most Holy
Archangels, help us
to persevere
in the Faith.
Instruct us in the
wisdom of the Saints,
and aid us in
our good works.

Ninth Choir:
O Most Holy Angels,
watch over
every human soul,
guiding and
protecting us,
and leading
us to Heaven.

Sixth Choir:
O Invincible Powers,
guard us from
the forces of darkness
and protect us
from the temptations
of pride, anger,
and impatience.

Seventh Choir:
O Sovereign
Principalities,
help us to grow
in the spirit of true
and sincere obedience.
Assist those who
are dying, and protect
our Parishes.

O my Guardian Angel,
remain always
at my side, to light,
to guard, to rule,
and to guide.

O Angel of
the Apocalypse,
may we be prepared
when the time comes
for you to blow your
trumpet and fulfill
God's Holy Plan!

*"Therefore, behold
I will allure her,
and will lead her into
the wilderness: and
I will speak to her heart."*
— Hosea 2:14

Cloistered Nuns, hidden behind walls and separated by grilles, embrace the centuries-old traditional Monastic Life. It is Jesus Himself Who has called and chosen each one of His Brides to live for Him alone.

Eight years of discernment will pass before each Nun professes the Solemn Vows of Obedience, Chastity, the renunciation of possessions, and the observance of Papal Enclosure. These Vows give the Nuns the freedom to be filled with the joy that Jesus promised to those who leave everything to follow Him. United by their love for Jesus, the Nuns live their Community Life in a family spirit, helping each other to grow in holiness.

At the Holy Sacrifice of the Mass, the pilgrim will hear the voices of the Nuns singing their praises to the Lord.

" . . . *you are to make sacred vestments to give dignity and magnificence . . .*
They must use gold, purple stuffs, violet shade and red, crimson stuffs, and fine twined linen."
—*Exodus* 28:2, 5

The Extern Sisters, like the Cloistered Nuns,
consecrate their lives to the Perpetual Adoration of Our
Lord Jesus Christ in the Most Blessed Sacrament. They are
called "Extern" because they live and work in a section
of the Monastery that is outside the Enclosure.
Representing the Monastic Community to the public, it is
the Extern Sisters who prepare for Mass, greet visitors
and pilgrims, and care for the Sanctuary and public side
of the Temple.

The Holy Sacrifice
of the Mass

Leaving the distractions of the world behind, the pilgrim is ready to enter into the central act of Worship of the

Catholic Church, the Holy Sacrifice of the Mass. When the Priest offers the Sacrifice at the Altar, we are privileged to

be at Calvary. The Father's great Attribute of Omnipresence, meaning that everything is present to God, enables us to

be truly present beneath the Cross of Jesus as He is immolated in reparation to the Father for the sins of the world.

We are privileged to be called by the Father to be present at that awesome moment, for the Father sees us along with

Our Lady, Saint John, and Saint Mary Magdalene as we behold His Son dying on the Cross.

   The Torches, Incense, and Prostration are acts of solemn Worship of Jesus. Prostration is an external sign

of the soul's self-offering and Worship of God alone. At the Temple, it is performed as an act of reparation for

the irreverences, blasphemies, and sacrileges committed against Our Lord's Real Presence in the Most

Blessed Sacrament.

*This shield covers the Monstrance during the celebration of the Eucharist, turning the pilgrims' attention to the Altar and the Holy Sacrifice of the Mass. Immediately after Mass, the shield is lowered while the Nuns chant their Motto, "**Adoremus in Aeternum**", to resume the day's Adoration.*

Saint Francis of Assisi spent entire nights in prayer repeating the words: ***"DEUS MEUS ET OMNIA" ("My God and my All!")***. This Latin inscription appears above the Nuns' Cloister Communion Grille that separates the Sanctuary from the Nuns' Mass Chapel.

At the Consecration of the Mass, six of the Nuns prostrate themselves upon the inlaid marble floor which bears the inscription ***"+ SANCTUS + SANCTUS + SANCTUS" ("Holy, Holy, Holy")***. This act of profound Adoration and Worship is a venerable tradition of the Poor Clare Nuns of Perpetual Adoration.

This is the Mystery of our Faith!

"In awe should all men tremble, the whole earth quake, and the heavens shout for joy, when Christ, the Son of the Living God, is Present upon the Altar in the consecrated hands of a Priest! Such awesome grandeur! Such wondrous condescension! O sublime humility! O humble sublimity! God and the Son of God, the Almighty Lord of the universe, deigns to humble Himself, meekly hiding under the tiny form of bread for our salvation! See, my brothers, the humility of God, and pour out your hearts before Him! Humble yourselves, that you may be exalted by Him. And keep back for yourselves nothing of yourselves, but give yourselves totally, to the One Who gives Himself totally to you" (Saint Francis of Assisi).

As the Priest says the words of Consecration at Mass, the bread ceases to be bread and is turned into the Body of Christ, and the wine is turned into the Blood of Christ. This total change of the bread and wine is called **Transubstantiation**. It is no longer bread, but the Body of Christ. It is no longer wine, but the Precious Blood of Christ. The awesome Body and Blood, Soul and Divinity of Jesus are present before us.

Jesus said to His Apostles, "I will not leave you orphans." For two thousand years, He has been in our midst in the Eucharist as Saviour, Friend, and Lord. The deepest union possible on this earth between God and the soul occurs during the reception of Holy Communion.

When we receive the Holy Eucharist, Jesus comes to dwell in our soul and we become sharers of the Divine Nature (2 Peter 1:4).

"Heavenly Father, when Your Priest holds up the Host and says, 'Corpus Christi', let my soul bow in humble Adoration before the love and humility of Jesus. Let my heart be a pure resting place for Your Son."

— Mother M. Angelica

The mosaic of the Pelican on the front of the Main Altar is a symbol of the Holy Eucharist dating back to the beginnings of Christendom. Jesus feeds us with His very Own life-giving Blood, flowing from His Most Sacred Heart.
"I am the bread of life. He who comes to Me will never be hungry; he who believes in Me will never thirst" *(John 6:35).*

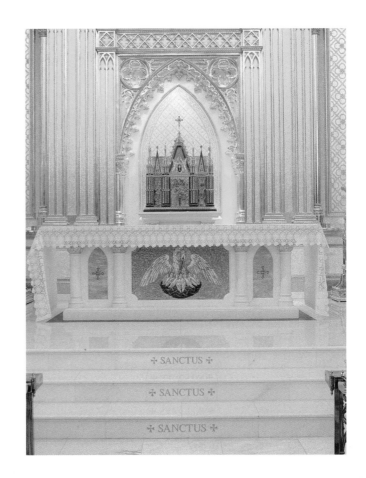

I devoutly adore Thee,
O Hidden God,
truly hidden beneath these appearances.
My whole heart submits to Thee
and in contemplating Thee,
it surrenders itself totally . . .

I do not see Thy Wounds as Thomas did,
but I confess that Thou art my God.
Make me believe more and more in Thee,
hope in Thee, and love Thee always . . .

O Lord Jesus, Loving Pelican,
wash me clean with Thy Blood,
one drop of Which
can free the entire world of all its sins . . . .

Excerpts from Saint Thomas Aquinas' "Adoro Te Devote"

65

The loving, compassionate Face of the Eternal Father looks down toward His children in the Temple from the West Rose Window. Majestically portrayed in a gesture of benediction, He is ready to welcome and embrace every penitent soul who seeks to return to his Father's House.

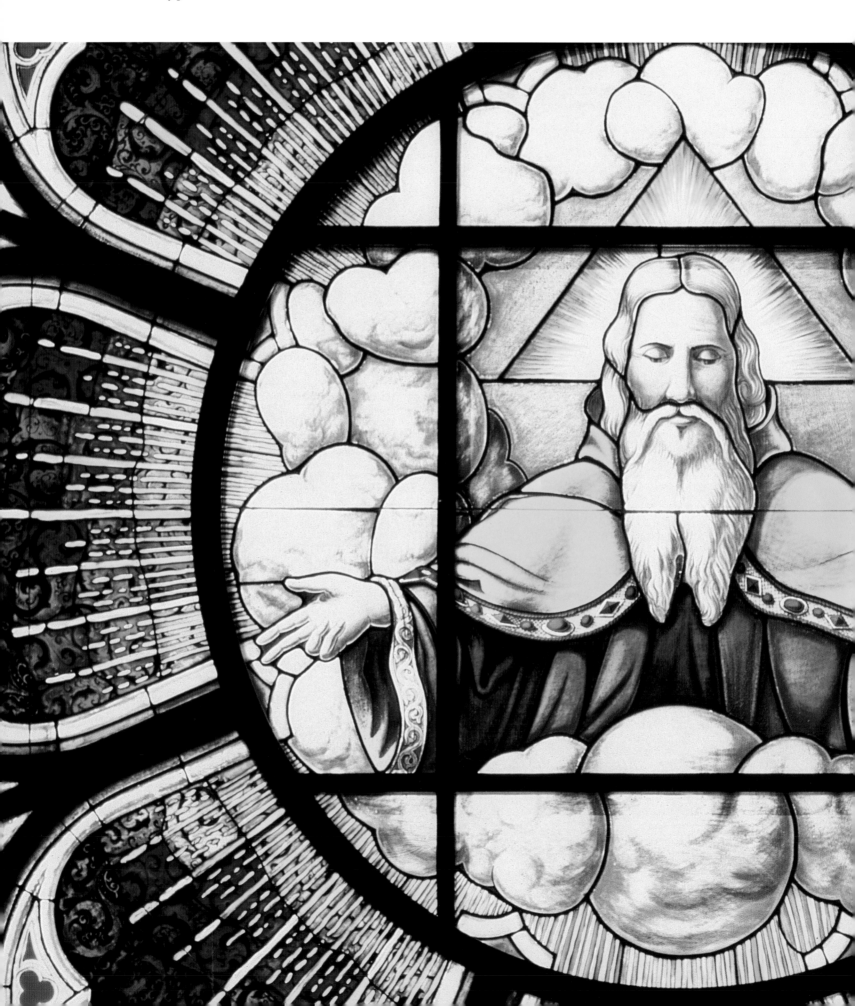

"Think of the love that the Father has lavished on us,
by letting us be called God's children; and that is what we are."
— 1 John 3:1

Jesus promised to send the Holy Spirit. *"The Advocate, the Holy Spirit, Whom the Father will send in My Name, will teach you everything and remind you of all I have said to you. Peace I bequeath to you, My own peace I give you, a peace the world cannot give, this is My gift to you. Do not let your hearts be troubled or afraid" (John 14:26-27).* The Holy Spirit has guided the Church through the ages and continues His work of sanctifying souls.

"Come, Holy Spirit, fill the hearts of Thy faithful, and enkindle in them the Fire of Thy Love!"

"No sooner had He come up out of the water than he saw the heavens torn apart and the Spirit, like a dove, descending on Him."

— *Mark 1:10*

"Now a great sign appeared in Heaven; a Woman, adorned with the sun, standing on the moon, and with the twelve stars on her head for a crown."
— *Revelation 12:1*

As He was dying on the Cross, Jesus gave us His Mother Mary to be our own Mother. It is through her maternal hands that we receive the graces necessary to be faithful to Jesus. She is a loving Mother always ready to help her children.

A pilgrimage made under the loving gaze of Mary will draw the soul into a closer union with her Divine Son Jesus.

My Queen and my Mother, remember that I am thine own. Keep me, guard me, as thy loving child.

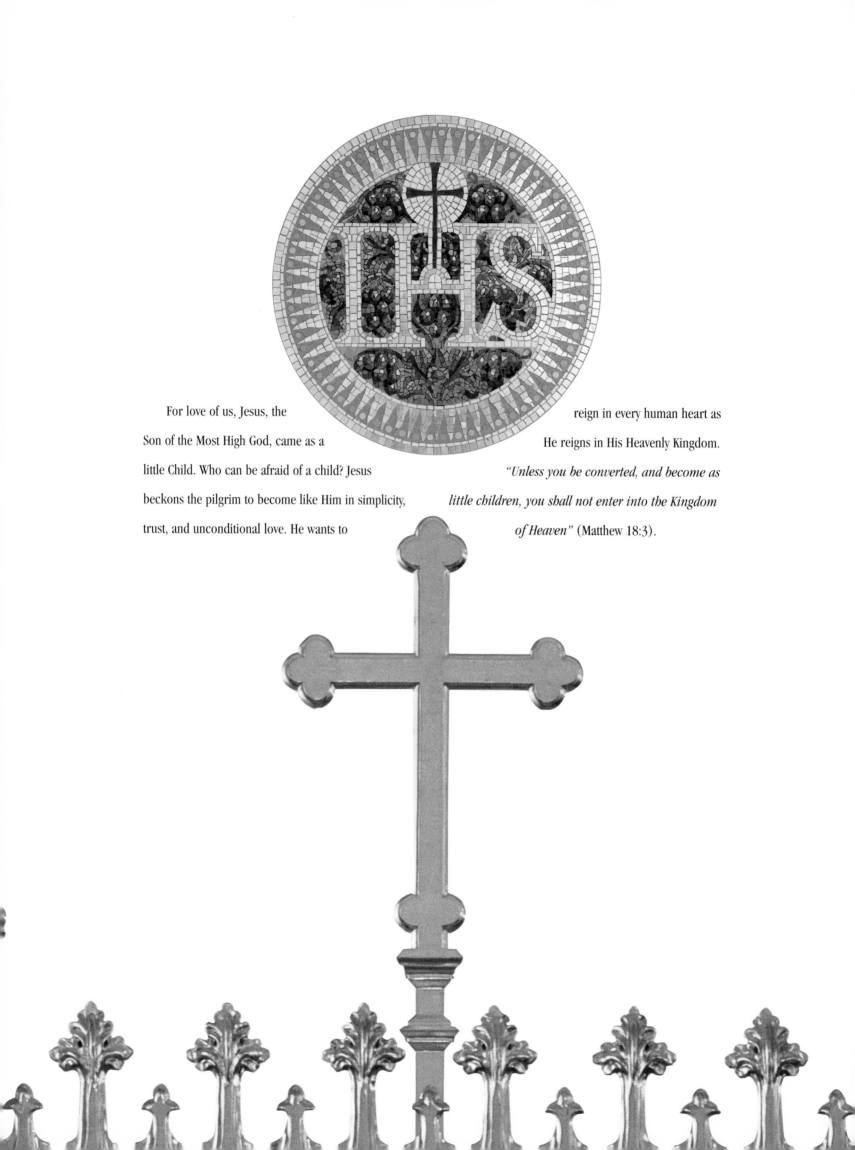

For love of us, Jesus, the Son of the Most High God, came as a little Child. Who can be afraid of a child? Jesus beckons the pilgrim to become like Him in simplicity, trust, and unconditional love. He wants to reign in every human heart as He reigns in His Heavenly Kingdom. *"Unless you be converted, and become as little children, you shall not enter into the Kingdom of Heaven"* (Matthew 18:3).

The Annunciation

"Hail, Full of Grace, the Lord is with thee." — Luke 1:28

Sweet Virgin of Nazareth, when the darkness of sin covered mankind,

your love and humility turned the Face of the Father toward

His erring children. Though the message of the Angel was difficult for

you to understand, you accepted the Will of God with trust and love.

O Mary, your trust in the Father's Will made the miraculous simple.

Why can't I trust His Plan in my life as you trusted Him in yours?

Give me a share, I beseech you, of your Faith and Hope that I may

bow before the Infinite Wisdom of God and accept the treasures

He deigns to bestow upon my soul.

79

The Visitation

"When Elizabeth heard the greeting of Mary, the babe leaped in her

womb; and Elizabeth was filled with the Holy Spirit."

— Luke 1:41

O Mary, what impulse of love made you hurry to visit

your cousin Elizabeth? At a moment when you had every right to rest

in the jubilant news that you would be the Mother of the Messiah,

you left the place of your exaltation. Obtain the graces I need to

magnify the Lord by humility and charity in dealing with my neighbour,

concern for the aged and the unborn, zeal for social justice, and

unfailing courage when duty calls for sacrifice.

The Adoration of the Magi

"And going into the house they saw the Child with His Mother Mary,

and falling to their knees they did Him homage. Then, opening their

treasures, they offered Him gifts of gold and frankincense and myrrh."

— Matthew 2:10-11

Dear Infant Jesus, I want to take my place

with the Magi in Adoration, giving You the gold of my love,

the frankincense of my prayers, and the myrrh of my sacrifices.

Teach me how to worship You "in Spirit and in Truth" (John 4:23),

to the glory of the Father. I desire to follow Your example, my Infant

King, as You reached out to the Wise Men from the East. Help me to rise

above all prejudice and love my neighbour as You love me.

The Hidden Life

"He went down with them and came to Nazareth,

and was obedient to them; and His Mother kept all these things

in her heart. And Jesus advanced in wisdom, and age,

and grace with God and men."

— Luke 2:51-52

O Jesus, for thirty years You lived a hidden life at Nazareth,

obedient to Mary and Joseph. As You worked faithfully as a carpenter,

help us to be faithful to the duties of our state in life.

Teach us the value of humility and obedience. Grant us the grace

to be thoughtful, joyful, and loving in our own families.

The Resurrection

"He has risen!" "Alleluia!"

— Matthew 28:6; Apocalypse 19:1

Most Holy Redeemer, the joy of Your Resurrection

fills my soul with exultation and the realization that my body, too,

will rise some day. The Wisdom of the Father will be glorified forever,

as all men see how His Plan and Will in my life marked out the glory

that would be mine for all Eternity. All my trials and sufferings will

seem as nothing compared to the glory Your sufferings merited for me.

The vision of Your Face will fill my soul with exquisite joy.

The Ascension

"Then He took them out as far as the outskirts of Bethany,

and lifting up His hands He blessed them. Now as He blessed them,

He withdrew from them and was carried up to Heaven."

— Luke 24:50-51

Glorified Jesus, I find the day You ascended to the Father a sad day.

Teach me to prefer consoling You to being consoled.

Give me the light to exercise my Faith when all seems dark.

I want to rise above the demands of my emotions

and have the courage to live in Spirit and Truth.

Grant me the Faith that is always aware of the invisible reality,

the Hope that trusts Your Promises, and the Love that seeks not itself.

The Descent of the Holy Spirit

"And suddenly there came a sound from Heaven . . . and there appeared

to them parted tongues . . . and they were all filled with the Holy Spirit."

— Acts 2:2-4

Holy Spirit, like those in the Upper Room before Pentecost,

I am often timid, fearful, and confused. I beg You to pour out

an abundance of Your Gifts upon me, that I may be strong, courageous,

and enlightened. O Sanctifier of my soul, give me an awareness of the

Divine Indwelling and a realization of how much the Father loves me.

Transform my soul into the perfect image of Jesus.

The Assumption and Coronation of the Blessed Virgin

She is the brightness of eternal light, and the unspotted mirror of God's Majesty, and the image of His Goodness. — Wisdom 7:26

Sweet Mary, my Queen, what comfort I find in knowing that you are in Heaven as my Mother with all the love and concern your dignity demands. Help me to always rise above the things of earth so my thoughts may be with you in Heaven. Your Assumption and Coronation fill my soul with assurance. Your heart was pierced with Seven Sorrows during your earthly pilgrimage, but now twelve stars encircle your head and the moon is under your feet (Revelation 12:1). Never allow this thought to part from me, especially when the cares of this world weigh heavily upon my shoulders.

Hail, Holy Queen

Hail, Holy Queen, Mother of Mercy,
our life, our sweetness, and our hope!
To thee do we cry, poor banished
children of Eve.
To thee do we send up our sighs,
mourning, and weeping
in this valley of tears.
Turn, then, Most Gracious Advocate,
thine eyes of Mercy toward us,
and after this our exile,
show unto us
the Blessed Fruit of thy womb,
Jesus.
O Clement, O Loving, O Sweet
Virgin Mary!

Pray for us, O Holy Mother of God,
that we may be made worthy of the
promises of Christ.
Amen.

God has created each soul with a great desire and capacity for holiness. The more the soul advances in the spiritual life, the more it recognizes the hindrances to holiness.

"Come to Me, all you who labour and are overburdened, and I will give you rest" (Matthew 11:28). The ultimate goal of every pilgrimage is conversion. At the Temple, many souls find the opportunity to break away from sin once and for all. Devout participation at Mass, spiritual talks, and quiet moments of prayer lead to true conversion of heart. Enkindled with the desire to receive the Lord's Mercy, the pilgrim is inspired to make a humble and life-changing Sacramental Confession. Freed from its burden of sin, the soul then experiences the delight of renewed friendship with God, and exults in the fruits of joy and peace.

"Precious Blood of Jesus, purify my soul, make my conscience sensitive to sin, make my heart humble and docile, and wash away all my sins and faults. Present me one day to Your Father as a perfect image of You!"

— Mother M. Angelica

When Our Lord reigns as King, then true freedom is found. In order to live this glorious freedom from sin, Jesus must be our Teacher, Lord, and Ruler. To remind the pilgrim of this, there is an image of Jesus as Pantocrator (a Greek word meaning Ruler or Teacher) carved on the Vestibule in the rear of the Temple.

An exact photographic replica of the Holy Shroud of Turin, located in the marble Antechamber of the Lower Church, provides the pilgrim with material for reflection. To the skeptic, the Holy Shroud represents an unsolved mystery. But to the believer, it is the very burial cloth of Our Lord Jesus Christ.

Turin has been the proud home of the actual Shroud since 1578. It was there that the Shroud was photographed for the first time in 1898. To the astonishment of all, the image that appeared on the negative was a positive image, much clearer than the actual image on the Holy Shroud. Both the negative and the positive images of the Holy Shroud are displayed here at the Temple.

The Holy Shroud reveals many details of Our Lord's Passion, Death, Burial, and Resurrection. Prayerful pondering of these images leads the pilgrim to reflect on the true meaning of life, death, and Eternity. Most moving, especially in the negative image of the Holy Shroud, is the marvelous image of the Holy Face of Jesus, revealing an unearthly peace and beauty. This countenance could never have been created by any artist's hand, for it is the Face of the Son of God.

By meditating on the Sufferings of Jesus as seen in the images of the Holy Shroud, pilgrims are inspired to live their lives in a way that is pleasing to God, so that one day they may be with Jesus in Paradise and love Him for all Eternity.

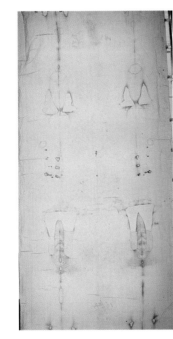

*"It was now evening, and since it was Preparation Day (that is, the vigil of the Sabbath), there came Joseph of Arimathea, a prominent member of the Council, who himself lived in the hope of seeing the Kingdom of God, and he boldly went to Pilate and asked for the Body of Jesus . . . [Pilate] granted the Corpse to Joseph **who bought a Shroud, took Jesus down from the Cross, wrapped Him in the Shroud and laid Him in a Tomb** which had been hewn out of the rock." — Mark 15:42-47*

The Temple, or Upper Church, is reserved for silent prayer and Adoration. The only services celebrated in the Upper Church are the daily Conventual Mass of the Nuns, their recitation of the Holy Rosary, and the chanting of the Divine Office (the Liturgy of the Hours). All other services for pilgrims take place in the Lower Church.

Pilgrims may pray before the Tabernacle in the Lower Church and visit the Crypts of the deceased Nuns. At **Benediction of the Most Blessed Sacrament**, the Priest places the Holy Eucharist within a Sacred Vessel called a Monstrance (from the Latin word meaning to

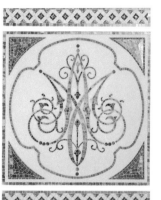

show or display). Here the pilgrim has the privilege of honoring the Blessed Sacrament with *"the veneration and adoration that is due to God Himself, as has always been the practice recognized in the Catholic Church"* (*Eucharistiae Sacramentum*, 1973, #3). Hymns, prayers, and a homily are included. Then the Priest lifts the Monstrance and blesses the people. This devotion *"stimulates the faithful to an awareness of the marvelous Presence of Christ and is an invitation to Spiritual Communion with Him"* (*Instruction on Eucharistic Worship*, 1967, #60).

"My good and dear Jesus, I kneel before You, asking You most earnestly
to engrave upon my heart a deep and lively Faith, Hope, and Charity, with true repentance for my sins,
and a firm resolve to make amends. As I reflect upon Your Five Wounds,
and dwell upon Them with deep compassion and grief, I recall, Good Jesus,
the words the Prophet David spoke long ago concerning Yourself:
They have pierced My Hands and My Feet, they have counted all My Bones!"
(Psalm 21:17). Crucifix on the wall of the Lower Church.

"O Mary, conceived without sin, pray for us who have recourse to thee." Statue of Our Lady in the Lower Church.

*"Then Jesus told His disciples,
'If any man would come after Me,
let him deny himself and take up
his cross and follow Me.'"*
— Matthew 16:24

By living the Gospels in total simplicity, Saint Francis learned the secret of "perfect joy". It is not when life is painless and all our desires are fulfilled that we possess perfect joy. Only when we accept our crosses with serenity do we find the joy that no one can take away.

Saint Francis loved to meditate on the Sufferings of Jesus, and is often depicted with a Crucifix in his hand. Two years before the Saint's death, Jesus imprinted upon his body the Sacred Stigmata, the marks of Jesus' Own Wounds. Francis had become a living, visible portrait of the Crucifixion, a sign of hope and joy for every soul.

"My Jesus, You saw beauty in the Cross and embraced it as a desired treasure. Help me to trust the Father and to realize that there is something great behind the most insignificant suffering. There is Someone lifting my cross to fit my shoulders — there is Divine Wisdom in all the petty annoyances that irk my soul every day. Teach me the lessons contained in my Cross, the wisdom of its necessity, the beauty of its variety, and the fortitude that accompanies even the smallest cross" (Mother M. Angelica).

Saint Clare is usually portrayed holding a Monstrance. The city of Assisi was threatened by the Saracens, but Clare could not rise from her sickbed. She had the Nuns bring her to the doorway, and with the Monstrance in her hands, she prayed: *"Defend, I beseech Thee, O Lord, these Thy handmaids whom I myself am unable to defend at this hour!"* Instantly a voice was heard in reply, like the voice of a little child, coming from the Sacred Host: *"I will always defend you!"* Suddenly the enemy fled in terror, and the entire city was saved. Today the Poor Clare Nuns, spiritual daughters of Saint Clare, continue to pray for the needs of all who request their prayers.

ENCLOSURE

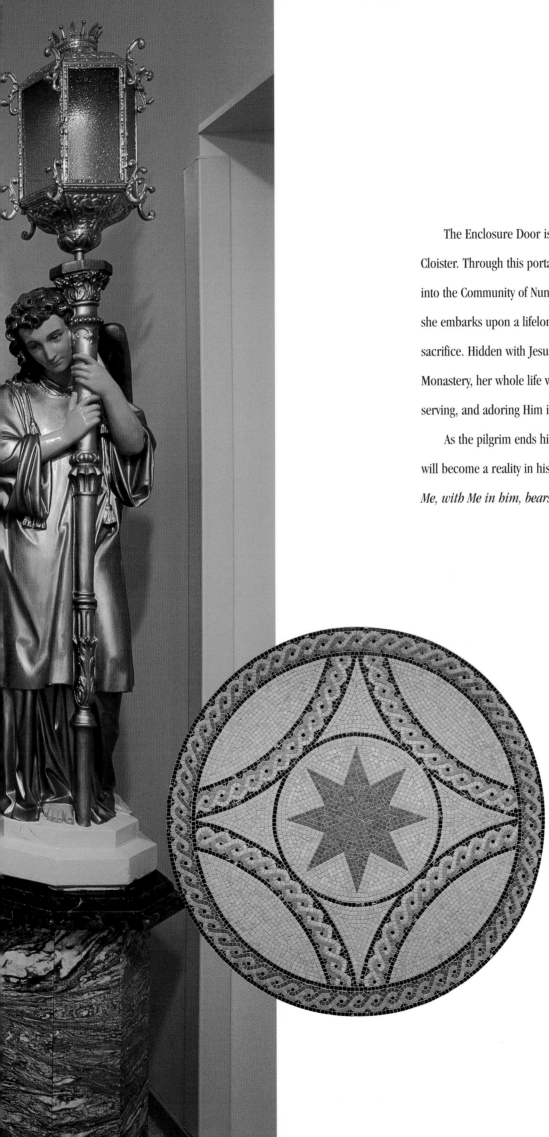

The Enclosure Door is the entrance into the Cloister. Through this portal, each new Sister is admitted into the Community of Nuns. In crossing this threshold, she embarks upon a lifelong pilgrimage of prayer and sacrifice. Hidden with Jesus inside the walls of the Monastery, her whole life will be consecrated to loving, serving, and adoring Him in the Most Blessed Sacrament.

As the pilgrim ends his journey, the promise of Jesus will become a reality in his life: *"Whoever remains in Me, with Me in him, bears fruit in plenty"* (John 15:5).

*Deo gratias
per Jesum in
Sanctissimo Sacramento!*

*Thanks be to
God through Jesus in the
Most Blessed Sacrament!*

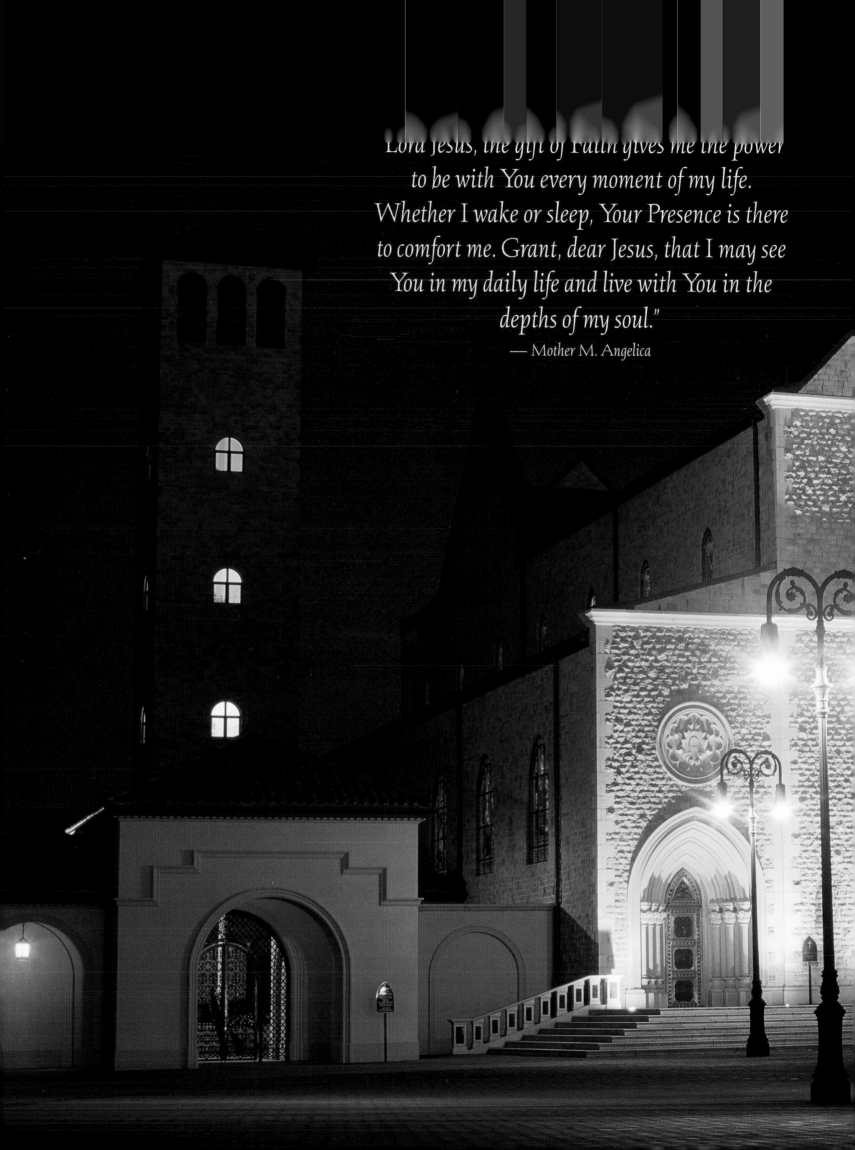

Lord Jesus, the gift of Faith gives me the power
to be with You every moment of my life.
Whether I wake or sleep, Your Presence is there
to comfort me. Grant, dear Jesus, that I may see
You in my daily life and live with You in the
depths of my soul."

— Mother M. Angelica

Front Cover Angels adoring the Most Blessed Sacrament. This Shield is a hand-painted wood panel that is raised to cover the Monstrance during the Holy Sacrifice of the Mass. ©2001 Hugh Hunter

p. 1 Traveling on the long road leading to the Temple, pilgrims have time to put the cares of the world behind them and prepare their hearts to enter into the Presence of Our Eucharistic King.©2000 Hugh Hunter

p. 2/3 The approach to the Temple. The Temple and Monastery are located in Hanceville, Alabama on an isolated tract of farmland that is almost completely surrounded by a river. ©2000 Hugh Hunter

p. 6 Mother M. Angelica, Foundress and Abbess of Our Lady of the Angels Monastery, stands near the statue of the Divino Niño Jesús in the Cloistered Divine Office Chapel of the Nuns. ©2001 Hugh Hunter

p. 7 Bronze bas-relief of Saint Clare of Assisi holding the Monstrance (see pictorial description of page 33 for additional details). ©2001 Hugh Hunter

p. 10 Illuminated Manuscript: excerpts from Psalm 84 and Ecce Panis Angelorum in Gregorian Chant. Gothic Textura Quadrata Calligraphy and Illumination by the Poor Clares of Perpetual Adoration. ©2001 Bill Freeman

p. 11 Praying the Rosary. ©2001 Bill Freeman

p. 12/13 Aerial view of the magnificent Temple and Monastery. The architectural style was inspired by the great Franciscan Churches and Monasteries of the 13th Century, especially those of Assisi and the region of Umbria in Italy. Brice Building Company, Inc., General Contractors, of Birmingham, Alabama is responsible for the construction of the Temple and Monastery. Chosen by Mother Angelica after much thought and prayer, Brice Building Company worked closely with her at every stage of the project. Mother Angelica finalized every decision, from the greatest to the least significant. Brice coordinated the work of all specialized sub-contractors including the European firms chosen by Mother Angelica and the Nuns. The Romanesque-Gothic appearance of the entire edifice was achieved using both traditional and modern materials and techniques. Some techniques had to be devised on-site. The Project Managers of Brice and their team of expert foremen, craftsmen, and laborers have accomplished a remarkable feat in completing this structure and all its ornamentations. Mother Angelica and the Nuns are deeply grateful to Brice Building Company and to everyone who worked on this monumental project. ©2000 Hugh Hunter

p. 14/15 The Piazza is the size of approximately two-and-a-half football fields (259' by 289'). English Tudor-style pavers border the Piazza and Colonnade. The central herringbone pattern of the Piazza was painstakingly laid by American and Brazilian craftsmen. Simpson Commercial Contracting, Inc. of Birmingham, Alabama framed the arches and ceiling vaults in the Colonnade, and did the stucco work and ornamentation of the Colonnade. The clay roof-tiles used on the Temple, Colonnade, and Monastery were fabricated and fired in Colombia. ©2001 Bill Freeman

p. 15 Children easily relate to the Statue of the Divine Child Jesus atop the Monument in the Piazza. ©2001 Bill Freeman

p. 15 The Scripture quotation engraved on the steps of the Monument, ". . . And a little Child shall lead them" (Isaiah 11:6), appears in four languages – Spanish, German, Italian, and English – each one chosen because of that country's contribution to the construction and adornment of the Temple. All interior appointments in the Temple were designed and fabricated in Spain. The Stained-glass Windows were created in Germany. Marble and granite were cut in Italy and assembled by expert local craftsmen from Alabama in the U.S.A. ©1999 Bill Freeman

p. 16/17 Monument of the Divine Child Jesus in the Piazza, designed by TAG (Talleres de Arte Granda, S.A., of Madrid, Spain) and assembled by Masonry Arts, Inc. of Bessemer, Alabama. The granite was fabricated by Savema, S.P.A. of Pietrasanta, Italy. Sculpted in Italy of statuary white marble from Carrara, the statue of the Child Jesus was commissioned by Masonry Arts, Inc., and is patterned after a small plaster statue made by the Cloistered Carmelite Nuns of Madrid, Spain. His Heart is carved of Red Jasper. ©1999 M. Lewis Kennedy, Birmingham, AL

p. 18/19 Statue of the Divine Child Jesus with the Father's Rose Window in the background. ©2001 Hugh Hunter

p. 20 The carillon's largest bell, named "Divino Niño Jesús", decorated for the formal Blessing Ceremony on the Feast of Saint Joseph the Worker, May 1, 1998. ©1998 Phil Arello

p. 21 The campanile (bell tower) houses a carillon of fourteen bells. Eleven bells, obtained from an older Church, were restored and retuned by the Verdin Company, Cincinnati, Ohio. Three new matching bells were cast to complete the musical scale. Each bell is engraved with a Saint's name. ©1999 M. Lewis Kennedy

p. 22 The Temple's Gothic facade, which faces the West, was patterned after the Basilica of Saint Francis in Assisi, with its geometric sections, Central Gothic Arch, and Rose Window. The smaller circle beneath the Tau Cross is a medieval-style ventilation port, covered with an ornamental wrought-iron grille.

The original Roman Cross mounted at the peak of this Temple's facade was altered when a fierce storm sheared off the upper portion, changing the Cross into the form of a Tau. Mother Angelica saw this as a manifestation of Divine Providence, and decided to leave it as a Tau Cross. A "Tau" Cross differs from a Roman Cross in that its vertical beam terminates at the horizontal beam, like the capital letter "T". The Franciscan Order, from its very beginnings, has been identified with the Tau Cross. At the Fourth Lateran Council in 1215, Pope Innocent III urged that the Tau be used throughout Christian Europe to signify prayer for renewal of the Church. Saint Francis adopted this symbol as his own signature. ©2000 M. Lewis Kennedy

p. 22 Alpha and Omega Rosettes above the bronze Minor Doors of Saint Francis and Saint Clare, hand-carved from Indiana Limestone. The Alpha and the Omega are the first and last letters of the Greek alphabet, recalling the words of Jesus in the Book of Revelation (22:13): *"I am the Alpha and the Omega, the First and the Last, the Beginning and the End."* ©2001 Hugh Hunter

p. 23 High above the bronze Great Doors, within the Central Gothic Archway, appears a limestone Rosette of two majestic Angels bearing a Shield. Engraved upon the Shield is the image of the Sacred Host with the Monogram of the Holy Name of Jesus, "IHS". Emanating from the Host are flaming rays of light, representing Jesus as the "Sun", the "Light of the world" (John 8:12). The renowned Franciscan Preacher, Saint Bernardine of Siena, was the pioneer in implementing this particular form of the IHS Monogram in spreading the Holy Name of Jesus across Italy. Below the Shield is a banner bearing the Nuns' Motto in Latin, "Adoremus in Aeternum Sanctissimum Sacramentum" ("Let us adore for all Eternity the Most Blessed Sacrament!"). ©1999 & 2001 M. Lewis Kennedy

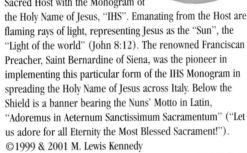

p. 24/25 The bronze Great Doors, commissioned by TAG (Talleres de Arte Granda, S.A., of Madrid, Spain). They are flanked by columns and corbel arches carved from limestone by Bybee Stone Company of Ellettsville, Indiana. The motif of the Great Doors is the Seven Joys and Seven Sorrows of the Blessed Virgin Mary. All doors and transoms are embellished with high-relief panels. The Great Doors with their quatrefoil (four-petal) panels resemble those of the famous Churches in Pisa, Florence, and Rome. ©2001 Hugh Hunter

p. 26, top Extern Sisters of the Poor Clares of Perpetual Adoration open the Great Doors. ©2001 Bill Freeman

p. 26, bottom The transom above the Great Door at the North side of the Central Gothic Archway depicts the first of the Seven Joys of Mary, The Annunciation. The Latin inscription translates as: "Virgin of the Seven Joys, your Son was born for us."©2001 Hugh Hunter

p. 27, top The transom above the Great Door at the South side of the Central Gothic Archway depicts the first of the Seven Sorrows of Mary, The Prophecy of Simeon. The meaning of the Latin inscription is: "Virgin of the Seven Sorrows, your Son died for us." ©2001 Hugh Hunter

p. 27, inset Decorative 13th-Century capitals designed by TAG (Talleres de Arte Granda, S.A., of Madrid, Spain). These capitals adorn all the columns of the facade. ©2000 Hugh Hunter

p. 28/29 The Rosary of the Seven Joys of the Blessed Virgin Mary, known as the Franciscan Crown, originated in the year 1422. It was the custom of a pious young man to adorn a certain statue of the Blessed Virgin with fresh flowers woven into a wreath, as a sign of his devotion and love. When he became a Franciscan Novice, he was no longer permitted to continue this devotion, and was tempted to leave the Order and return to the world. But as he knelt in prayer before her statue, Our Lady appeared to him in a vision. She told him to change his pious practice into one that would be more pleasing to her and more meritorious for his soul. She taught him how to weave a crown for her from the flowers of his prayers, which would always remain fresh and never wither. She disappeared, and the young Friar began to pray as she had taught him: one "Our Father" and ten "Hail Marys" in honor of each of her Seven Joys. As he prayed, the Novice Master came by and saw an Angel weaving a marvelous wreath of roses. After every tenth rose the Angel inserted a golden lily. When the wreath was finished, the Angel placed it upon the head of the Friar like a crown. The Novice Master asked the Novice the meaning of the vision, and was so amazed that he immediately shared this event with the other Friars. The recitation of the Crown of the Seven Joys of the Blessed Virgin Mary soon spread throughout the Franciscan Family. The Poor Clares at Our Lady of the Angels Monastery wear the Franciscan Crown Rosary as part of their Holy Habit. ©2001 Hugh Hunter

p. 30/31 The Devotion of the Seven Sorrows or Seven Dolours of Mary, an adaptation of the Holy Rosary, was instituted during the 13th Century. It was promoted by the Order of Servants of Mary, known as the Servites. This devotion recalls the sorrows that Our Lady endured in compassion for the Sufferings and Death of her Divine Son. The Seven Sorrows Devotion is prayed upon a Chaplet of seven times seven beads, each portion of seven being divided from the rest by medals that represent the seven principal sorrows of Mary's life. ©2001 Hugh Hunter

p. 32 The transom above the bronze Minor Door of Saint Francis, located at the North end of the Portico, featuring a relief of Saint Francis of Assisi, Founder of the three Franciscan Orders: the Friars Minor, the Poor Clare Nuns, and the Third Order of Saint Francis. The Franciscan Order is referred to as the "Seraphic Order" because of Saint Francis' ardent ("seraphic") love for Jesus Christ. It was in the form of a Seraph that Jesus appeared to Saint Francis two years before the Saint's death, imprinting upon his body the Sacred Stigmata (the Holy Wounds of Jesus). Saint Francis is depicted holding a Crucifix.

Gothic ornamental shields adorn the three quatrefoil (four-petal) high-relief panels on the bronze Minor Door of Saint Francis.

"We adore Thee, O Lord Jesus Christ . . .": Saint Francis of Assisi composed the first part of this prayer. In the tradition of the Poor Clares of Perpetual Adoration, the last phrase referring to the Most Blessed Sacrament is added at the end of the prayer. ©2001 Hugh Hunter

p. 33 The transom above the bronze Minor Door of Saint Clare, located at the South end of the Portico, depicting Saint Clare of Assisi. Co-Foundress of the Order of Poor Clares, she was the first woman to follow the ideals of Saint Francis. Saint Clare is the spiritual mother of all Poor Clare Nuns throughout the world. She is traditionally depicted as holding a Monstrance, recalling the miraculous intervention of Jesus in the Most Blessed Sacrament during the Saracen invasion (see p. 101).

As on the bronze Minor Door of Saint Francis, the three quatrefoil high-relief panels on the bronze Minor Door of Saint Clare are adorned with Gothic ornamental shields. ©2001 Hugh Hunter

p. 34/35 The pilgrim's first glimpse inside the spacious Temple. All interior appointments in the Temple, including the Monstrance, Tabernacle, Altars, Altar Rail, and Pews, were custom-designed and crafted by the master artisans of TAG (Talleres de Arte Granda, S.A., of Madrid, Spain). The hand-carved Reredos (the Sanctuary wall behind the Altar), located at the East end of the Sanctuary, is carved from rare Paraguay cedar and ornamented with 23-carat gold leaf. Soaring to a height of 55 feet above the Sanctuary floor, the Reredos separates the Main Church from the Cloistered Chapel of the Nuns (the "Divine Office Choir"). The Reredos houses the Tabernacle and draws the eyes upward to the

focal point of the Temple, the brilliant Monstrance where Jesus reigns on His Throne in the Most Blessed Sacrament.

Marble Floors/Sanctuary The floor surrounding the Main Altar is composed of rare Bianco Sivec marble from Macedonia, often referred to as "sugar marble" because its pristine whiteness glistens like sugar. Three steps lead from the Sanctuary floor to the Main Altar. Carved into the risers of these steps are the Latin words "SANCTUS, SANCTUS, SANCTUS" ("HOLY, HOLY, HOLY"), highlighted with gold leafing. The lower section of the Sanctuary floor includes Cremo Delicato marble from Carrara and Massa, Italy, with colorful geometric patterns of the same types of marble found in the Nave.

Marble Floors/Nave The Main Aisle of the Nave is paved with colorful inlaid marble designs in geometric patterns. TAG (Talleres de Arte Granda, S.A., of Madrid, Spain) designed all the patterns for the marble floors, while Masonry Arts, Inc. of Bessemer, Alabama coordinated the layout in conjunction with Savema, S.P.A. of Pietrasanta (near Carrara), Italy, where all the marble was cut, honed, and polished. Masonry Arts, Inc. of Bessemer, Alabama installed all the marble inside the Temple. The background field of the floor is of Cremo Delicato marble from Carrara and Massa, Italy. The two main designs featured on the marble floor are the Star of Bethlehem and the Cross, representing the Birth of Jesus and His Crucifixion. The Star of Bethlehem designs are cut from Cremo Valencia marble from Valencia, Spain, on a background of Cipollino marble quarried at Lucca, Italy. The Cross designs are comprised of genuine Red Jasper from Turkey, meticulously cut in a distinctive cross shape and accurately set to the four points of the compass, emphasizing Jesus' Kingship over the whole world.

Columns and Wainscot The tapered columns of this Temple have been faced with curved sections of Cremo Delicato marble from Carrara and Massa, cut by a sophisti-cated technique developed in Italy. Italian craftsmen are world-renowned experts in fashioning such tapered columns, which draw the eye upward toward Heaven. The square bases of the columns and the marble wainscot are adorned with inlaid marble of Breccia Pernice from Verona, Italy (marble insets); Verde Alpi Scuro from Aosta, Italy in the Italian Alps (marble borders); Cremo Delicato (back-ground field); and Botticino Classico marble from Brescia, Italy (foot of the column bases and wainscot).

The Gothic capitals of the columns were designed by TAG (Talleres de Arte Granda, S.A., of Madrid, Spain) and fabricated by Savema, S.P.A. of Pietrasanta, Italy.

Stained-glass Windows The East and West Rose Windows, the Great Windows in the Nave, and the Upper Nave Windows of the Holy Angels were all custom-made for the Temple by the studios of Gustav Van Treeck in Munich, Germany, in the centuries-old Bavarian style. The clear outer windows are made of a special glass with a wavy surface, which deflects the sun's rays and enhances the brilliance of the colors in the Stained Glass. This wavy glass was also imported from Germany, the only place where it is made.

Ceiling Vaults Churches have traditionally employed vaulted (arched) ceilings to visibly represent the inverted

Barque of Saint Peter. Due to the architectural characteristics of this Temple, the first attempt at forming the vaults was unsuccessful, and the ceiling of the Central Nave had to be dismantled. This caused considerable delay in the completion of the Temple. In a seemingly impossible feat, the specifications of the arched vaults were re-engineered by the master architect of TAG (Talleres de Arte Granda, S.A., of Madrid, Spain), to achieve the desired expansive and uplifting effect. These graceful, soaring vaults were expertly shaped and plastered by Simpson Commercial Contracting Inc. of Birmingham, Alabama. ©2000 M. Lewis Kennedy

p. 36/37 The magnificent Monstrance, in which Jesus in the Most Blessed Sacrament is perpetually exposed for Adoration, is the very heart of the Temple. The consultants of TAG (Talleres de Arte Granda, S.A., of Madrid, Spain) presented Mother Angelica and the Nuns with a century-old pattern for a small Monstrance which had never been executed. The blueprint had to be modified to scale the Monstrance to its height of almost eight feet, and to enable the Sacred Host to be seen from both the public side of the Temple and the Divine Office Choir where the Nuns maintain Perpetual Adoration.

Four cameos adorning the cross-shaped section of the Monstrance represent the six-winged Seraphim, the Choir of Angels that is constantly worshiping the Lord (cf. Isaiah 6:2 and Revelation 4:8). Flaming golden rays surrounding the Sacred Host represent the Shekinah, the "glory of the Lord" that filled the Temple (Exodus 40:35). The Monstrance in the Temple is surrounded by four wood-carved, hand-painted adoring angels representing the Cherubim of the Ark of the Covenant. The Mercy-Seat of the Ark of the Covenant in the Old Testament was a foreshadowing of Jesus truly Present in the Most Blessed Sacrament. In the Book of Exodus, the Lord God instructed Moses to make two Cherubim and set them upon the Mercy-Seat of the Ark of the Covenant, with their wings spread, looking towards each other, and their faces turned toward the Presence of the Lord (Exodus 25:18-22).

Crowning the Monstrance is the Reredos' gold-leafed wood cupola that houses Jesus' Eucharistic Throne. The light-ing of the Throne was engineered to maximize the brilliance of the Monstrance, drawing the eye toward His Real Presence in the Most Blessed Sacrament. ©2000 M. Lewis Kennedy

p. 38 The large gold Tabernacle behind the Main Altar in the Temple is cus-tom-designed and crafted by TAG (Talleres de Arte Granda, S.A., of Madrid, Spain) as a miniature Gothic Church. It is adorned with a Monstrance symbol on a maroon enamel background above the Tabernacle door. This Monstrance symbol was molded from the Habit Monstrance worn by Mother M. Angelica. Surrounding the Monstrance are two adoring Angels. Reliefs on the front of the Tabernacle depict the

Stations of the Cross in medieval art form. Hand-painted enameled columns frame the door and sides of the Tabernacle. Engraved on the inside of the Tabernacle door is a Shield bearing two adoring Angels and the inscription "Adoro Te Devote". ©2001 Hugh Hunter

p. 39, bottom ". . . And the glory of the Lord fills the Temple!" – adapted from Ezechiel 43:5.

p. 39, right Another TAG (Talleres de Arte Granda, S.A., of Madrid, Spain) creation, the Sanctuary lamp features a chain with enameled quatrefoil links. The lamp can be raised and lowered to facilitate changing the candle inside the red glass globe. Only genuine beeswax candles are used in this lamp. ©2001 Hugh Hunter

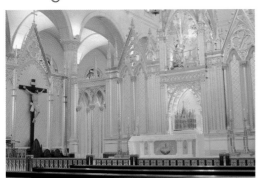

p. 40/41 Close-up of the Sanctuary and Reredos. The life-size Crucifix located to the North of the Sanctuary depicts Our Lord's Agony on the Cross. Mother Angelica asked TAG (Talleres de Arte Granda, S.A., of Madrid, Spain) to pattern this Crucifix according to the findings of studies of the Holy Shroud of Turin. The sign at the top of the Cross is a faithful representation of the original inscription ordered by Pontius Pilate, "Jesus of Nazareth, King of the Jews", in three languages: Hebrew, Latin, and Greek. ©2001 Hugh Hunter

p. 42/43 The Upper Nave Stained-glass Windows of the Holy Angels ("clerestory" windows in the upper portion of the walls above the aisle roofs). One Angel from each of the nine Choirs of Angels is depicted, as well as the Archangels Saint Michael, Saint Gabriel, and Saint Raphael. The last two windows at the North-East end of the Temple picture a Guardian Angel and the Angel of the Apocalypse. ©2001 Hugh Hunter

p. 44 A source of meditation even for little children, the Angels in the Stained-glass Windows capture the attention of all who visit the Temple. ©2001 Bill Freeman

Saint Michael is the Prince of all the Holy Angels. He is depicted in armour, holding his flaming sword and bearing a shield emblazoned with the Latin words, "QUIS UT DEUS", which means

"WHO IS LIKE UNTO GOD!" These symbols represent his victory in the battle against the devil and the rebellious angels (Jude 9, Revelation 12:7-9). The letter "U" in the inscription on the shield is formed like the letter "V", in accordance with the custom in the Roman Empire during the time of Our Lord Jesus Christ.

Saint Gabriel is the Archangel who is mentioned in Holy Scripture as the messenger of God who appeared to Daniel (the Book of Daniel, 8:15-27 and 9:20-27). He prophesied the time of the coming of Christ (Daniel 9:24-26). It was Saint Gabriel who appeared to Zechariah to foretell the birth of Saint John the Baptist (Luke 1:11-20). In the greatest and most joyful message ever given by God through an Angel to mankind, Saint Gabriel announced to the Blessed Virgin Mary that she would become the Mother of God (the Annunciation, Luke 1:26-38). It is possible that Saint Gabriel was also the Angel who appeared to the shepherds announcing the Birth of the Messiah at Bethlehem. Saint Gabriel's name means: Strength of God. He is usually depicted holding a lily, representing holy purity. Another representation of Saint Gabriel appears in the Temple's Great Window of the Annunciation (see p. 79). ©1999 Hugh Hunter

p. 45 Saint Raphael is the Archangel of the Book of Tobit. The name "Raphael" means "Medicine of God", recalling his miraculous assistance (both bodily and spiritual) to Tobit, Tobias, and Sara (the Book of Tobit). He is depicted holding a fish because of its healing properties (Tobit 6). Saint Raphael is honored for his gifts of wisdom and grace, and is often invoked for assistance as a guide to travelers, a consoler of the unfortunate, a deliverer from diabolic influence, and a refuge for sinners. His instructions to young Tobias before his wedding are the ideal of moral perfection for all married couples: prayer, continence, and pure intention. Following Saint Raphael's counsels, Tobias and Sara were rewarded with a long and happy marriage, in which they both saw their children's children to the fifth generation.

The Nine Choirs of Angels All the Nine Choirs of Angels are represented in the Upper Nave Windows of the Temple. The Nine Choirs have a hierarchical order, organized into three groups or "rings" of three Choirs each. The first group, consisting of the Seraphim, Cherubim, and Thrones, are directly concerned with the contemplation of God. This group is sometimes called the "Ring of Adoration". The second group, including the Dominations, Virtues, and Powers, are concerned with the universal government of the world, as Ministers of Divine Government. The third group, comprised of Principalities, Archangels, and Angels, is assigned to particular ministrations and missions dealing with the work of Redemption, the Church.

The Seraphim, the highest of the Choirs of Angels, stand at the Throne of God. They have more perfect knowledge of God than any other creature. The name "Seraphim" means "burning" or "glowing", representing the ardor and intensity of their love for the Most Holy Trinity. They are always depicted with six wings because of their description in Isaiah Chapter 6: "I saw the Lord Yahweh seated on a high Throne; His train filled the Sanctuary; above Him stood two Seraphs, each one with six wings: two to cover its face, two to cover its feet and two for flying" (Isaiah 6:2). The Seraph's mouth is open, signifying this Choir's unceasing singing of the praises of God: "Holy, Holy, Holy is Yahweh Sabaoth. His glory fills the whole earth" (Isaiah 6:3). The intensity of their ardent

devotion is revealed in verse 4, which demonstrates the power of their crying out in song: "The foundations of the threshold shook with the voice of the one who cried out, and the Temple was filled with smoke" (Isaiah 6:4). It was also a Seraph who purified the Prophet's tongue with fire – a burning coal (Isaiah 6:6). Saints whose lives have been completely ruled by the ardor of Divine Love are often called "Seraphic", such as Saint Francis of Assisi, Saint Teresa of Avila, and Saint Catherine of Siena.

The Cherubim, second of the Nine Choirs of Angels, are the Throne-bearers of Almighty God (Psalm 17:11, 79:2 and 98:1; Ecclesiasticus 49:10; Isaiah 37:16; and Ezechiel 10:1-21). They are also the heavenly custodians and protectors of holy places and sacred things. They were assigned by God to guard the way to the Tree of Life with a flaming sword when Adam and Eve were cast out from the Garden of Eden (Genesis 3). God commanded Moses to make beaten-gold images of two Cherubim in the Tabernacle, for the Throne of Mercy (the Ark of the Covenant: Exodus 25:10-22). Their name signifies their powerful knowledge of God and their contemplation of the Divinity.

The Thrones form part of the court of the Heavenly King, sharing with the Seraphim and Cherubim the sublime dignity of being closer to the Throne of God than all the other Choirs of Angels. They receive more of the light of the Mysteries of God than all the lower Choirs. Untainted by anything earthly, their name symbolizes the Kingship of Christ. ©1999 Hugh Hunter

p. 46/47 The Dominations rule over the three Angelic orders that are charged with executing the commands of the Divine Majesty. They have great zeal for maintaining the King's authority. The Dominations call to our minds God's universal sovereignty over all creatures, visible and invisible, emphasizing our ultimate end.

The Virtues are the Angelic Choir confided with carrying out the orders given by the Dominations. Because of their great strength, it is believed that many instances of heavenly intervention in Holy Scripture were performed by the Choir of Virtues. They help us to overcome our faults and sins.

The Angels of the Choir of Powers are appointed to do battle against the evil spirits who wage spiritual war against mankind. The Powers plan and direct the campaign against the forces of darkness. Examples of strength in meekness, they enlighten the lower Choirs in how the commands of the Divine Majesty are to be carried out. They are a favorite Choir among devout souls.

The Principalities preside over the last three of the nine Choirs. Like generals, they are God's immediate servants charged with ruling the visible world. Their duties include guarding the nations of the earth and persons of great importance, such as Pontiffs, Kings, and heads of Religious Orders.

The Archangels are entrusted with important missions to men. They are also given as guardians to those who have been entrusted with special work to do for God. It is believed that the seven Angels who stand before the Throne of God (Rev. 8:2) are from this Choir. They are associated with singing the praises of God, full of happiness and courage.

The Angels, the last of the nine Choirs, are sent as messengers to men. They mirror the goodness of God to all His creatures and exemplify the virtue of humility. They are believed to escort the Blessed Virgin Mary whenever she visits the earth, and to keep a constant vigil of Adoration wherever the Blessed Sacrament is kept.

A Guardian Angel is assigned by God to each soul at the moment of conception, indicating the tremendous value God places on our immortal souls. This Angel is always at our side, "to light, to guard, to rule, and to guide." They guide us as to God's Holy Will, and guard us from evil spirits. Ask your Guardian Angel, who was with Jesus during all the events of His Life, to help you meditate on the Life of Our Lord.

The Angel of the Apocalypse is mentioned in the Book of Revelation, Chapter 10, Verse 7: "But in the days of the voice of the seventh Angel, when he shall begin to sound the trumpet, the mystery of God shall be finished, as He hath declared by His servants the Prophets." In praying to the Angels of all the Heavenly Choirs, recall that each of these Angels took part in the Battle of Heaven and made an irrevocable choice to serve God alone, for all Eternity. ©1999 Hugh Hunter

p. 49 The Cloistered Divine Office Choir. Here is where the Cloistered Nuns observe their hours of Adoration of Jesus in the Most Blessed Sacrament around the clock, and where they chant the Divine Office, the official prayer of the Church. The Lectern is used for the Readings of the Divine Office. At the beginning of each Adoration Hour, pilgrims may hear the Nuns chanting the Magnificat prayer in alternating verses (Luke 1:46-55). After the Magnificat, the Adorer goes to the Lectern and recites an Adoration Prayer that is a tradition in the Order of Poor Clares of Perpetual Adoration.

Behind the Lectern, three marble steps lead up to the devotional Altar. Carved into the risers of these steps, and highlighted with gold leafing, are Latin words from the Roman Canon of the Holy Sacrifice of the Mass: "+ HOSTIAM PURAM + HOSTIAM SANCTAM + HOSTIAM IMMACULATAM +" ("PURE VICTIM, HOLY VICTIM, IMMACULATE VICTIM!", referring to Jesus' offering of Himself on the Altar). To the East of the Divine Office Choir is a Loggia for the Stations of the Cross leading into the other areas of the Cloister. ©2001 Hugh Hunter

p. 50 The Vestry, where Priests and Deacons vest for the Holy Sacrifice of the Mass, located behind the Altar of Our Lady of Grace. Extern Sisters set out the Vestments that the Priests will wear for Holy Mass. It is in this private room that the Priests prepare for Mass with a time of silent prayer. ©2001 Hugh Hunter

p. 50, inset An intricately hand-sewn Humeral Veil, which the Priest wears during Benediction of the Most Blessed Sacrament. ©2001 Hugh Hunter

p. 51, inset Sacred Vestments worn by Priests and Deacons during the Holy Sacrifice of the Mass. These beautiful Vestments give honor and glory to God as well as inspiring deeper reverence for the exalted dignity of the Priest, who celebrates Mass as an *alter Christus* – "another Christ". The Sacred Vestments, especially those that are more elaborate for special Solemnities and Feasts, are exquisitely embroidered with traditional devotional designs using materials that are worthy of being used in Divine Worship: the finest silks, lace, and gold threads. ©2001 Hugh Hunter

p. 52/53 Mass Procession in the Temple. This Temple was "consecrated", meaning that it can never be used as anything but a Catholic Church. In consecrated Churches, twelve gold Consecration Crosses are permanently mounted on the columns at places where there was a special anointing with Holy Chrism Oil by the Bishop. Two of these are visible in the photograph on the two columns at the sides of the Sanctuary. On the Anniversary of the Consecration, December 19, which is celebrated as a Solemnity each year, candles are placed into the twelve Crosses and remain lit throughout the day. ©2000 Hugh Hunter

p. 54/55 On Sundays and Feast Days, the Holy Sacrifice of the Mass is celebrated with greater solemnity. Here the server carries the Censer and container of incense that the Priest will use at certain parts of the Mass. From the earliest days of Christianity, incense has been used during the celebration of Mass, so that a fragrant, pleasing sacrifice would ascend to the Lord. ©2001 Hugh Hunter

p. 56, inset Hand-painted wood Shield depicting Angels adoring the Most Blessed Sacrament. This Shield covers the Blessed Sacrament during the celebration of the Holy Sacrifice of the Mass. ©2001 Hugh Hunter

p. 57 Act of prostration during the Consecration of the Holy Eucharist at Mass. "The twenty-four elders prostrated themselves before Him to worship the One Who lives for ever and ever, and threw down their crowns in front of the throne . . ." (Revelation 4:10). The ringing of the Sanctuary bells is a sign of the awesome moment of Transubstantiation. The bells are rung before the words of Consecration, immediately after the Consecration of the Body of Christ, and immediately after the Consecration of the Precious Blood of Christ, signaling the appropriate signs of reverence for the Holy Eucharist. ©2000 Hugh Hunter

p. 58 Inlaid marble floor design behind the Grille in the Cloistered Mass Choir. The center of this intricate design is an inlaid Red Jasper cross. The diagonal measurement between the smaller corner crosses is 22 feet. It is here that the Nuns prostrate during the Consecration of the Holy Eucharist at Mass. Prostration is an ancient Monastic tradition. During the ceremony of a Nun's Solemn Profession, the act of Prostration signifies the Nun's total self-offering to the Lord forever. ©2001 Hugh Hunter

p. 59 Grille separating the Cloistered Mass Choir from the Sanctuary. The Latin inscription of the prayer Saint Francis loved to pray, "DEUS MEUS ET OMNIA" ("MY GOD AND MY ALL!"), appears within the Gothic arch of the Grille. In this Mass Choir, located at the South end of the Sanctuary, the Cloistered Nuns attend Mass, make their thanksgiving after Mass, and recite the Holy Rosary. Four Stained-glass Windows adorn the Mass Choir: the Sacred Heart of Jesus, the Immaculate Heart of Mary, Saint Francis, and Saint Clare. ©2001 Hugh Hunter

p. 60 The Priest holding up the Sacred Host for the Adoration of the faithful, who pray in the words of Saint Thomas the Apostle: "My Lord and my God" (John 20:28). ©2001 Hugh Hunter

p. 62 Chalice (for the Precious Blood of Jesus) and Ciborium (receptacle for the Sacred Hosts) commissioned for the Consecration of the Temple in December 1999 and used only for special Solemnities and Feast Days. Both of these Sacred Vessels, adorned with enamels of a Monstrance symbol and of El Divino Niño Jesús, were designed and expertly crafted by TAG (Talleres de Arte Granda, S.A., of Madrid, Spain). ©1999 Marcus Peavy

p. 63 Communicants kneeling at the Altar Rail to receive Holy Communion. ©2001 Bill Freeman

p. 64 Mosaic of the Pelican on the front of the Main Altar. Crafted of pieces of glass and gold, the mosaic was commissioned by Masonry Arts, Inc. of Bessemer, Alabama, and created by artisans in Pietrasanta, Italy, using a 400-year-old method of hand-chiseling and fitting. ©1999 M. Lewis Kennedy

p. 65 "SANCTUS, SANCTUS, SANCTUS" ("HOLY, HOLY, HOLY") carved into the risers of the Sanctuary steps leading to the Main Altar, highlighted with gold leafing. These words are from the Holy Sacrifice of the Mass, immediately preceding the Eucharistic Prayer. ©2001 Bill Freeman

p. 66/71: The Three Divine Persons of the Most Holy Trinity are prominent in the Temple: the Eternal Father, Jesus truly Present in the Most Blessed Sacrament, and the Holy Spirit. During the three years of preparation for the Great Jubilee of the Year 2000, each year was dedicated to one of the three Divine Persons. By Divine Providence, a significant component of the Temple was completed during each of these years, corresponding to the Divine Person to Whom that year was dedicated.

p. 66/67 The Father's Rose Window, located directly above the bronze Great Doors, was completed in 1999, The Year of the Father. ©1999 Hugh Hunter

p. 68 Photograph showing the Dove from the Rose Window of the Holy Spirit centered in the cross-shaped opening above the Monstrance. The Monstrance was completed in 1997, The Year of Jesus. ©2001 Hugh Hunter

p. 69/70/71 The Holy Spirit Rose Window, located in the Nuns' Divine Office Chapel. It can be viewed when entering the Temple's Main Entrance. This Window was completed in 1998, The Year of the Holy Spirit. ©1999 Hugh Hunter

p. 72 Devotional Side Altar of Our Lady of Grace, located on the North side of the Temple near the Vestry. Our Lady bears a magnificent crown and a halo of twelve stars. This comforting statue invites silent prayer to the Blessed Virgin Mary, the Mother of Jesus. ©2001 Hugh Hunter

p. 73, right Close-up of the serene face of the statue of Our Lady of Grace. ©1999 Bill Freeman

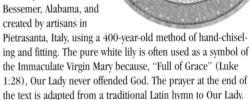

p. 73, center Mosaic of the lily at the front of the Side Altar of Our Lady. Crafted of pieces of glass and gold, the mosaic was commissioned by Masonry Arts, Inc. of Bessemer, Alabama, and created by artisans in Pietrasanta, Italy, using a 400-year-old method of hand-chiseling and fitting. The pure white lily is often used as a symbol of the Immaculate Virgin Mary because, "Full of Grace" (Luke 1:28), Our Lady never offended God. The prayer at the end of the text is adapted from a traditional Latin hymn to Our Lady. ©1999 M. Lewis Kennedy

p. 73, bottom Detail of the Gothic spires adorning the top of the Reredos (Sanctuary panel). All the adornments of the Reredos are hand-carved from rare wood and gold-leafed by hand. ©2000 Hugh Hunter

p. 74/75 View of the Side Aisle and Devotional Side Altar of El Divino Niño Jesús at the South side of the Temple. The marble bases of the columns feature quatrefoil (four-petal) designs (see notes to pages 34/35). These colorful designs are reflected in the geometric patterns of the inlaid marble paving. Atop each column is a Gothic capital. The beautifully proportioned, brightly-illumined vaulted ceiling creates a sense of spaciousness and light. ©1999 M. Lewis Kennedy

p. 76 Mosaic at the Side Altar of El Divino Niño Jesús. Crafted of pieces of glass and gold, the mosaic was created by artisans in Pietrasanta, Italy, using a 400-year-old method of hand-chiseling and fitting. The "IHS" in this mosaic, the first three letters of the Holy Name of Jesus in the Greek language, is a traditional symbol for Jesus. The Holy Name is often invoked as a powerful weapon in spiritual combat. With a childlike trust in Our Lord – Whose Arms are ever ready to embrace us and Whose Omnipotent Strength is ever ready to defend us – we should invoke His Holy Name and have confidence in His unfailing Love. The grapes are a symbol of the True Vine and of the Precious Blood of Jesus. ©1999 M. Lewis Kennedy

*p. 76, **bottom*** Detail of one of the gold-leafed, wood-carved Crosses atop the Reredos. ©2000 Hugh Hunter

p. 77 Statue of El Divino Niño Jesús, the Divine Child Jesus, at the South Devotional Side Altar in the Temple. Holding out His Arms, He is interceding with His Father for all of us. The face of the statue depicts the gentle, loving, and serene countenance of El Divino Niño Jesús. The wood-carved, hand-painted statue was made by the artisans of TAG (Talleres de Arte Granda, S.A., of Madrid, Spain). ©2001 Hugh Hunter

p. 78/83 The Great Windows All the Stained-glass Windows in the Temple come from the studios of Gustav van Treeck in Munich, Germany, where they were custom-drawn, painted, and fired with the traditional Munich-style methods used for centuries by the finest Bavarian glassmakers. Each window features a colorful border. The canopy at the top of each Great Window portrays stonework with four statues in relief, with intricate background patterns above the canopy. The clear outer windows are made of a special glass with a wavy surface, which deflects the sun's rays and enhances the brilliance of the colors in the Stained Glass. This wavy glass was also imported from Germany, the only place where it is made. The subjects represented in the series of Great Windows are from the Joyful and Glorious Mysteries of the Holy Rosary. Meditations by Mother Angelica.

p. 79 The Annunciation: Mary of Nazareth is shown kneeling in prayer when the Angel Gabriel appears to her and announces that she is to be the Mother of the Messiah

(Luke 1:26-38). The Holy Spirit shines upon her, and she conceives Jesus in her womb while remaining a perpetual Virgin. ©2000 Hugh Hunter

p. 80, left: The Visitation: The Blessed Virgin Mary, with Jesus in her womb, went in haste to visit Saint Elizabeth, the expectant mother of Saint John the Baptist (Luke 1:39-56). The background scene includes elements to be found in the typical Jewish household of the First Century. ©2000 Hugh Hunter

p. 80, right: The Adoration of the Magi: The Blessed Virgin Mary and Saint Joseph adore the newborn Infant Jesus, while the three Kings of the East bow down and worship Him, bearing gifts of gold, frankincense, and myrrh. The Star which led them to Jesus is depicted under the canopy (Matthew 2:9-11). ©2000 Hugh Hunter

p. 81, left: The Hidden Life: The Holy Family (Luke 2:51-52) at work in their home at Nazareth. The Boy Jesus assists His foster-father Saint Joseph in carpentry tasks. The Blessed Mother is shown with the spindle. ©2000 Hugh Hunter

p. 81, right: The Resurrection: Jesus rises in glory from the Tomb. At the left, an Angel adores the Risen Lord, while the guards fall to the ground at Jesus' feet. In the distance at the far right, the tiny figures of the three women can be seen on their way to the Tomb (Luke 24:1-11). ©2000 Hugh Hunter

p. 82, left: The Ascension of Jesus into Heaven: Our Lady and the Apostles look on in wonder as Jesus returns in glory to Heaven (Luke 24:50-53). ©2000 Hugh Hunter

p. 82, right: The Descent of the Holy Spirit: The Apostles were gathered with Our Lady in prayer in the Cenacle (the Upper Room of the Last Supper), when suddenly the Holy Spirit descended upon them in the form of tongues of fire (Acts 2:1-5). ©2000 Hugh Hunter

p. 83 The Assumption and Coronation of the Blessed Virgin: After her earthly life came to its conclusion, the Blessed Virgin Mary was taken into Heaven body and

soul, to be crowned as Queen of Heaven and Earth by the Most Holy Trinity. The Eternal Father is depicted at the right, holding a scepter. Jesus, bearing His Cross, holds out her crown, and the Holy Spirit hovers over Them. The two Angels are shown bearing Our Lady into the Heavens. She is revealed as the Woman Clothed with the Sun, and with the moon under her feet (Revelation 12:1). At the bottom of the window is her tomb, filled only with lilies. The Apostles, after seeing a strange light above her tomb, opened it but did not find her body. ©2000 Hugh Hunter

The "Hail, Holy Queen" prayer is said at the end of the recitation of the Holy Rosary.

p. 84 The use of the traditional enclosed Confessional has recently been reaffirmed in an Instruction from the Holy See, guaranteeing the privacy of the penitent as an aid to a complete and worthy Confession. The four Confessionals in the Temple are hand-carved in Gothic style, from a rare cedar that grows only in Paraguay. This view shows part of the Temple's marble wainscoting, including a quatrefoil (four-petal) design between the two Confessionals. ©2001 Hugh Hunter

p. 85 The Stations of the Cross are fourteen scenes of the Sufferings of Jesus as He carried His Cross to Mount Calvary. They are exquisitely hand-painted by the artisans of TAG (Talleres de Arte Granda, S.A., of Madrid, Spain). The Stations of the Cross are prayed by walking from Station to Station while reciting prayers and meditating on each scene. ©1999 Hugh Hunter

p. 86/87 The Vestibule, just inside the entrance to the Temple, is made of rare cedar from Paraguay. Intricately carved by the artisans of TAG (Talleres de Arte Granda, S.A., of Madrid, Spain), the Vestibule features a relief of Jesus the Pantocrator (a Greek word meaning Ruler or Teacher). The function of the Vestibule is to help preserve the atmosphere of silent prayer in the Temple by shielding the passage to the doorways. ©2001 Hugh Hunter

p. 87 Detail of the marble paving of the Temple. Colorful geometric designs emphasize the orientation of the Temple and Monastery, set squarely on the four points of the compass as a reminder to pray for the entire world. Marble was selected from several countries and fabricated in Italy by the Savema Company in conjunction with TAG (Talleres de Arte Granda, S.A., of Madrid, Spain) who made the design, and Masonry Arts, Inc. of Bessemer, Alabama who reassembled and installed all the marble in the Shrine.

The inlaid crosses are of Red Jasper, measuring 34 inches across. The overall design is eight feet wide. Jasper is a semi-precious stone from Turkey, one of the materials mentioned in the Book of Revelation for the foundation of the Heavenly Jerusalem (Revelation 21:19). The frames around the cross are of Breccia Pernice marble from Verona, Italy on a background of Cipollino marble quarried at Lucca, Italy. The long, delicate points of the star-shaped design, representing the Star of Bethlehem, are of Cremo Valencia marble from Valencia, Spain. The border is of Verde Alpi Scuro from Aosta, Italy in the Italian Alps. ©2001 Hugh Hunter

p. 88 The Grand Stairway leading to the Lower Church and photographic replica of the Holy Shroud of Turin. Pilgrims may contemplate the marks of the Sufferings of Jesus on the Holy Shroud before entering the Lower Church, where they may pray silently before the Tabernacle. All pilgrim Masses, Holy Hours, and other services are held in the Lower Church. Behind the last pews are the Crypts of the deceased Nuns. ©2000 Hugh Hunter

p. 89 The Crucifixion Scene above the Grand Stairway is a high-relief panel made exclusively for the Shrine of the Most Blessed Sacrament by TAG (Talleres de Arte Granda, S.A., of Madrid, Spain). Our Lady, Saint Mary Magdalene, and Saint John, the Beloved Disciple, stand at the foot of the Cross mourning Our Saviour's Death. The skull is a reminder of our own death, an exhortation to repent of our sins, ask God's forgiveness, and live a holy life. ©2000 Hugh Hunter

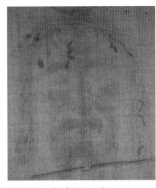

p. 90 The Holy Shroud of Turin. This permanent exhibit at the entrance to the Lower Church is an exact photographic replica of the actual Shroud of Turin. The four lighted panels reproduce both the positive and negative photographic images, positioned to permit close study. The numbers at the edges of the panels enable viewers to locate specific markings on the image. ©2001 Hugh Hunter

p. 92 Lower Church: Adoring Angels surround the Tabernacle where the Blessed Sacrament is reserved. Because of the Presence of Jesus in the Most Blessed Sacrament, pilgrims are asked to maintain continual silence in the Lower Church. ©2001 Hugh Hunter

 p. 93 Lower Church: Benediction of the Most Blessed Sacrament. After the Monstrance is placed on the Altar, the Priest swings the Censer to honor Jesus with clouds of incense. A mosaic with the A/M (Ave Maria) symbol of Our Lady appears on the face of the Altar in the Lower Church. Crafted of pieces of glass and gold, the mosaic was commissioned by Masonry Arts, Inc. of Bessemer, Alabama, and created by artisans in Pietrasanta, Italy, using a 400-year-old method of hand-chiseling and fitting. The first quotation is from Eucharistiae Sacramentum, a 1973 document of the Sacred Congregation for Divine Worship, #3.

The second quotation, #60 from Instruction on Eucharistic Worship, was issued in 1967 by the Sacred Congregation of Rites. ©2000 & 2001 Hugh Hunter

p. 94/95 Lower Church: Benediction. The Priest blesses the people with the Most Blessed Sacrament in the Monstrance. ©2001 Hugh Hunter

p. 96/97 Lower Church: the wall Crucifix, depicting Jesus dying on the Cross. ©2001 Hugh Hunter

p. 98/99 Lower Church: statue of Our Lady depicting her Immaculate Conception. ©2001 Hugh Hunter

p. 100 Lower Church: statue of Saint Francis of Assisi meditating on the Passion of Jesus. Saint Francis is wearing the traditional Franciscan Habit consisting of a brown robe with a cape and hood, a knotted cord, and a Rosary. His hair is cut in the usual form of a "tonsure", in which the crown of the head is shaved. ©2001 Hugh Hunter

p. 101 Lower Church: statue of Saint Clare of Assisi, Foundress of the Order of Poor Clares and spiritual mother of all Poor Clare Nuns in the world. She is shown holding the Monstrance, recalling how Jesus in the Most Blessed Sacrament drove away the Saracen invaders. Saint Clare is the Patroness of Television because of another miraculous event: bedridden for many years, she was too ill to attend Midnight Mass one Christmas Eve. While the other Nuns went to their Chapel for Mass, Saint Clare was transported in spirit to the Church of Saint Francis where his Friars were having their celebration. She could see everyone and hear all the hymns, even receiving Holy Communion from Jesus Himself. Later, when the Nuns came back to her room lamenting her absence at their beautiful Mass, she told them about the Mass she had "seen", including the details of the Sermon. It is due to this miraculous event that Pope Pius XII proclaimed Saint Clare the Patroness of Television. The miraculous words of Jesus, "I will always defend you!", are quoted from "The Legend and Writings of Saint Clare of Assisi", The Franciscan Institute, St. Bonaventure, NY, 1953, p. 34. Used with permission. ©2001 Hugh Hunter

p. 102 The Enclosure Door: entrance to the Cloister or "enclosed" area of the Monastery. It is locked with a special key, and can only be opened from the inside. There is no handle on the outside of the door. Two Angels bearing torches flank the doorway. Above the door is a lunette containing a relief of Saint Clare of Assisi, the spiritual mother of all Poor Clares, holding a Monstrance. It is at this door that each new Sister begins her Religious Life. ©2001 Hugh Hunter

p. 103 Detail of an inlaid Italian marble mosaic at the Enclosure Door. ©2001 Hugh Hunter

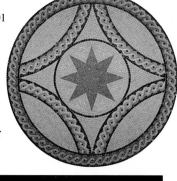

p. 104/105 The Shrine at night. Quotation adapted from Mother M. Angelica's "Ad Lib with the Lord", pocket edition, page 139: Faith. ©2001 Bill Freeman